BURGEROLOGY

THE FORMS & FLAVORS OF DELICIOUS BURGERS

©2016 The Companion Group

Berkeley, California

800-521-0505

www.companion-group.com

TABLE OF CONTENTS

Intro	v
How to Use a Burger Press	vi
Burger Grilling Products & Accessories	viii

Classic Burgers

Salmon Burger with Mango Salsa	1
Pepper Jack Avocado Burger with Haystack Onions	3
Sriracha Chicken Burger with Cabbage Slaw	5
Blue Cheese BLT Burger with Avocado Aioli	7
Curry Burgers with Pickled Fennel & Cilantro	9

Stuffed Burgers

Stuffed Banh Mi Burger	10
Cheddar Stuffed Burger with Onion Rings & BBQ Sauce	13
Pineapple Jalapeño Stuffed Jerk Burger	15
Stuffed Mediterranean-Style Burger with Tzatziki	17
Mushroom & Roasted Pepper Stuffed Burger	19

Mini Slider Burgers

Beef Sliders with Mushrooms & Smoked Gouda	21
Buffalo Chicken Sliders with Crispy Shallots	23
Bacon 'N Egg Breakfast Sliders with Chipotle Mayo	25
Hoisin Pork Sliders with Asian Slaw	27
Caramelized Onion & Swiss Sliders	29

INTRODUCTION

Some people say the best things are found in small packages. Some theorize that discovering a hidden treasure is the most rewarding. And yet others are happiest with the simple things in life.

In this book, all three types of people can find what they're looking for – and all of it can be found between two buns! Burgers, the American cuisine staple, have come a long way from your basic grilled patty, bun, and condiments. Now these handheld meals come in different shapes, sizes, and of course flavors.

In Burgerology, we explore the different permutations of patties: traditional burger patties, sliders, and stuffed burgers. Each has its own appeal. Sliders are a perfect party food, ready to be picked up and devoured in a few bites. On the opposite end

of the spectrum, stuffed burgers can satisfy even the biggest appetites, and are infused with the flavors of the ingredients contained inside. But of course, nothing beats a classic patty topped with all your favorite fixings.

The burgers in this book also play with influences from other cuisines. Burgers are versatile in that they require only a patty (made from any meat, or even veggies) held between two buns (of any kind of bread, or even no-carb veggie wrappers). Beyond that, you're free to take your favorite flavors from any part of the globe and bring them to your burger. Here, we borrow from South and East Asia, the Caribbean, the Mediterranean, Latin America, and different regions of the United States in order to inspire flavor combinations you wouldn't expect in your average burger. These fusions result in delicious meals you can create right at home.

These new combinations of burger form and flavor will inspire you to explore even further – a journey that's sure to be a delicious one.

HOW TO USE THE 3-IN-1 BURGER PRESS

We recommend using the Charcoal Companion® 3-in-1 Burger Press for best results. The 3-in-1 set contains one large ring with press for perfect classic burgers, and one small ring with press for bite-sized sliders. To make stuffed burgers, use a combination of the large ring and the small press to create patties with space for delicious fillings to go in between.

CLASSIC BURGER PATTY:

Place the large ring on a flat, food-safe surface and fill with 4 to 8 oz. of ground meat. Insert the large, handled press top into the ring and press down firmly. Remove the press and the ring to reveal the patty.

SLIDER PATTY:

Repeat process above using the small sized ring and press, with only 2 to 3 oz. of ground meat.

 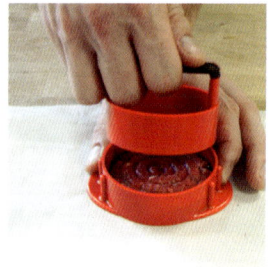

STUFFED BURGERS:

Fill the large ring with 8 oz. of ground meat. Use the large-sized press to create the first layer, then place the small-sized press top in the center of the patty and press down on the meat to create a well.

Remove the small press top and fill the well with your ingredients. Place 4 oz. more ground meat on top, and use large press top to compress and seal the patty. Remove the press top and the ring to reveal your patty. Check that the fillings are sealed inside. Crimp edges if needed before cooking.

 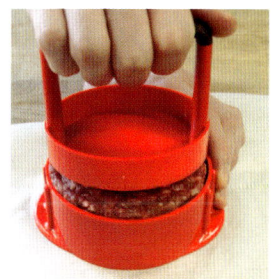

a twist on American CLASSICS

These burger baskets, serving accessories, and other products can make easy work of acheiving the perfect burger experience, every time.

3-in-1 Burger Press
Create burgers, sliders, or stuffed burgers with one press! This all-in-one press allows you to create burgers of different sizes or with the toppings on the inside. The large press and ring are the perfect size for a classic hamburger; the small press can make bite-sized sliders; and when used together the presses can create a well in your patty to stuff with delicious fillings.

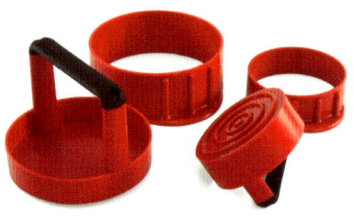

Barbecue Serving Set
Serve your burgers in classic outdoor American style: baskets, paper liners, and a set of ketchup and mustard squeeze bottles make it a meal.

Slider Basket
This basket holds nine sliders for easy grilling!

Cast Iron Round Grill Press
This cast iron grill press is great for smashing your classic burger patties. It has a raised ridge pattern on the bottom and helps to put impressive grill marks on your food.

Hamburger Grilling Basket
This burger basket allows you to grill and flip four hamburgers at once.

Stuff-A-Burger® Basket This basket is designed for extra-thick stuffed burgers and allows you to grill and flip four stuffed burgers at once.

SALMON BURGER WITH MANGO SALSA

A lighter choice with a touch of the tropical, this burger sweetens the buttery, umami-flavored salmon with a bright salsa made of mango, onion, and serrano chile.

Ingredients:
1 lb. salmon
1 egg
1 c. panko breadcrumbs
¼ c. yellow onion, minced
1 tsp. salt
1 tsp. pepper
2 brioche buns
Olive oil, as needed for cooking

Salsa:
1 medium sized mango
¼ c. red onion, finely diced
1 serrano chile, seeded, finely diced
2 Tbsp. cilantro, chopped
½ tsp. salt
½ tsp. sugar
1 Tbsp. olive oil
1 Tbsp. lime juice

Method:

Begin by removing skin from salmon and dicing it into ¼ inch cubes. Place cubes into a food processor with egg, breadcrumbs, yellow onion, salt and pepper and pulse 3 or 4 times until finely chopped.

Peel and dice mango into small cubes. Peel onion and mince into small pieces. Split serrano chili in half, remove most of the seeds and mince into small pieces. Combine all salsa ingredients in a bowl and mix to combine.

Form salmon into patties using patty press and grill 3-4 minutes per side or until patties are cooked to desired doneness. Serve with mango salsa and desired condiments.

Yield: 2 burgers

PEPPER JACK AVOCADO BURGER WITH HAYSTACK ONIONS

Pepper jack cheese provides the kick, fried haystack onion rings bring the crunch, and slices of ripe avocado bring it all together with their rich creaminess – this is a burger that will satisfy every taste and texture desire!

Ingredients:

1 lb. ground beef, 85/15%

2 tsp. garlic, minced

2 Tbsp. yellow onion, grated

Salt and pepper, to taste

1 medium avocado

2 slices pepper jack cheese

2 brioche buns

Olive oil, as needed for cooking

Haystack onions:

1 small red onion, sliced thinly into rings

1 c. buttermilk

1 c. all-purpose flour

1 c. light olive oil, for frying

Method:

Place meat in a medium bowl with garlic, yellow onion, salt, and pepper. Mix well to combine all ingredients. Form meat into patties using press and season with a light sprinkling of salt and pepper.

Slice red onion into thin rings. Pour buttermilk into a small bowl. Dredge onions in flour, place into the buttermilk, then dredge again in flour. Place olive oil in a sturdy-bottomed pan and preheat olive oil to 375°F. Once the oil is hot, fry the onions in 2-3 batches until golden brown. Season with a light sprinkling of salt immediately after cooking.

Brush patties with olive oil and grill 5-6 minutes per side or until desired doneness is achieved, melting cheese during the last 30 seconds of cooking. Serve on toasted buns with sliced avocado, fried onions, and desired condiments.

Yield: 2 burgers

SRIRACHA CHICKEN BURGER WITH CABBAGE SLAW

Cabbage slaw with a red wine vinegar marinade and a Sriracha basting sauce liven up a chicken burger with their tang and spice – this memorable burger is one to crow about!

Ingredients:

1 lb. ground chicken, dark meat
2 slices jack cheese
Kosher salt, to taste
Pepper, to taste
2 whole wheat buns
Olive oil, as needed for cooking
Cilantro, as needed

Basting sauce:

¼ c. Sriracha hot sauce
2 Tbsp. honey
¼ tsp. ginger powder

Slaw:

1 c. purple cabbage, shredded
1 c. green cabbage, shredded
3 Tbsp. red wine vinegar
1 tsp. sugar
¾ tsp. salt

Method:

Combine all slaw ingredients in a medium-sized non-reactive bowl, mix thoroughly, and allow to marinate at least 30 minutes before preparing patties. Combine all basting sauce ingredients in another small non-reactive bowl and mix thoroughly to combine.

Using the burger press, form two patties with the ground chicken. Season with salt and pepper. Brush patties with olive oil and cook over high heat 5-6 minutes per side or until 160°F internally, brushing with the basting sauce each time you flip the patties. Melt cheese during final 40 seconds of cooking. Serve topped with slaw on whole wheat buns.

Yield: 2 burgers

BLUE CHEESE BLT BURGER WITH AVOCADO AIOLI

This burger has a lot more going on than your average BLT. Pungent blue cheese balances the crisp freshness of the lettuce and tomato, and a creamy avocado aioli tempers salty strips of bacon.

Ingredients:

1 lb. ground beef, 85/15%

¼ avocado

1 tsp. lemon juice

3 Tbsp. organic mayo

½ c. blue cheese, crumbled

6 strips Black Forest bacon

2 leaves romaine lettuce

1 medium tomato, sliced

Onion powder, to taste

Garlic powder, to taste

2 cheese rolls

Olive oil, as needed for cooking

Method:

Form patties using press and season each side lightly with garlic and onion powder. Cook bacon in a sturdy-bottomed pan until done, set aside. Mash avocado in a small bowl, add mayo and lemon juice, and stir until fully mixed. Grill patties 5-6 minutes per side or until desired doneness is achieved. Heat bacon gently on the grill over medium flame until hot. Serve burgers on toasted cheese rolls with bacon, blue cheese, lettuce, tomatoes, onion, and aioli.

Yield: 2 burgers

CURRY BURGERS WITH PICKLED FENNEL AND CILANTRO

Fragrant curry powder brings extra dimension to these burgers, rounding out a hearty base to a light topping of thinly-sliced fennel and chopped cilantro. Get a slightly earlier start on this recipe to allow for the time needed to truly bring out the best flavors of your burgers' toppings!

Ingredients:

- 1 lb. ground beef, 85/15%
- 1 ½ Tbsp. curry powder
- 2 slices mozzarella cheese
- ½ bulb fennel, shaved thinly
- 2 Tbsp. apple cider vinegar
- ½ tsp. sugar
- 1½ tsp. kosher salt
- 1½ Tbsp. turmeric
- ¼ c. mayonnaise
- 2 Tbsp. cilantro, roughly chopped
- 2 sesame buns
- Olive oil, as needed for cooking

Method:

Slice fennel thinly using a mandolin or knife, and place in a non-reactive bowl with vinegar, sugar, and ½ tsp. salt. Toss thoroughly to coat. Allow fennel to sit at least 30 minutes for flavor to develop. Mix turmeric with mayonnaise and set aside.

Place ground beef in a mixing bowl and add curry powder and one tsp. of salt. Mix well to combine. Form patties using press and lightly season with pepper. Brush patties with olive oil and grill 5-6 minutes per side or until desired doneness is achieved, adding cheese during the last 30 seconds of cooking to melt. Serve on toasted buns with fennel, turmeric mayo, and cilantro.

Yield: 2 burgers

STUFFED BANH MI BURGER

This great Vietnamese sandwich is actually a mixture of Vietnamese and French food influences. We're adding a third: American barbecue. The result is more substantial than a traditional Banh Mi, but just as delicious.

Ingredients:

- ¼ c. carrot, grated
- ¼ c. daikon, grated
- ¼ c. jalapeno, chopped
- 1 Tbsp. rice vinegar
- ¼ c. fresh cilantro, chopped
- 1½ lb. ground pork
- 1½ tsp. fish sauce
- ½ Tbsp. fresh garlic, chopped
- ¼ c. cucumber, sliced
- 2 Tbsp. mayonnaise
- 2 baguette-style buns

Method:

Make slaw by combining carrot, daikon, jalapeno, rice vinegar, and cilantro in a small bowl. Set aside.

Combine ground pork, fish sauce, and garlic in mixing bowl, using hands to mix thoroughly. To form burgers, place ½ lb. of pork mixture into the ring of the burger press. Use the classic press to form the base patty, then push the slider press into the patty to form a well. Stuff the burger with ¼ cup of the slaw prepared earlier. Place ¼ lb. of ground pork mixture on top of the stuffing and use the classic press to seal. Cook burgers over direct heat until desired doneness is reached. Serve on a bun garnished with mayonnaise, sliced cucumbers, more slaw, and fresh cilantro.

Yield: 2 stuffed burgers

CHEDDAR-STUFFED BURGER WITH ONION RINGS AND BARBECUE SAUCE

Ride off into the sunset with this sky-high, stick-to-your-ribs burger. This burger is stuffed with chopped onions, crumbled bacon, and sharp cheddar – then topped with more! A slathering of sweet barbecue sauce finishes off the Western flavor profile.

Ingredients:

- 1 small yellow onion, chopped
- 1 Tbsp. olive oil
- 1½ lb. ground beef, 85/15%
- 2 Tbsp. barbecue sauce
- 4 oz. cheddar cheese, grated
- 6 strips of bacon, cooked
- 4 onion rings, cooked
- 2 hamburger buns

Method:

Heat a small sauté pan and add olive oil. Add chopped onions and cook over medium heat, stirring occasionally, until thoroughly caramelized. Season with salt and pepper to taste and set aside to cool. Crumble two strips of bacon and set aside.

Combine ground beef and barbecue sauce in a mixing bowl, using hands to mix thoroughly. To form burgers, place ½ lb. of ground beef mixture into the ring of the burger press. Use the classic press to form the base patty, then push the slider press into the patty to form a well. Stuff the burger with 2 oz. of cheddar cheese, 1 Tbsp. crumbled bacon, and 2 tsp. caramelized onions. Place ¼ lb. of ground beef mixture on top of the stuffing and use the classic press to seal. Cook over direct heat until thoroughly cooked. Serve burger on bun garnished with more barbecue sauce, bacon, and onion rings.

Yield: 2 stuffed burgers

PINEAPPLE JALAPEÑO-STUFFED JERK BURGER

The combination of sweet grilled pineapple and spicy charred jalapeños fill these pork burgers with punch! This Jamaican-inspired burger is best enjoyed on a sunny day with a light breeze – or whenever you want to transport yourself to one!

Ingredients:

2 pineapple rings, grilled
2 jalapeño peppers, grilled
1 shallot, chopped
1 garlic clove, chopped
½ c. fresh cilantro, chopped
½ c. sour cream
2 Tbsp. fresh lime juice (divided)
1½ lbs. ground pork
1½ Tbsp. jerk seasoning
¼ c. chopped green onions
2 crusty hamburger buns

Method:

Preheat grill to medium-high flame. Grill pineapple rings and jalapeño peppers until they begin to char. Chop pineapple into large chunks and set aside. Remove the stem and seeds of the jalapeños, chop roughly, and set aside. Make a dressing by adding the shallot, garlic, cilantro, sour cream, and 1 Tbsp. of fresh lime juice to a blender or food processor. Combine until smooth. Transfer to a container and refrigerate until ready for use.

Combine ground pork, jerk seasoning, and remaining 1 Tbsp. lime juice in mixing bowl, using hands to mix thoroughly. To form burgers, place ½ lb. of ground pork mixture into the ring of the burger press. Use the classic press to form the base patty, then push the slider press into the patty to form a well. Stuff the burger with 2 Tbsp. chopped grilled pineapple, 1 Tbsp. jalapeño, and 1 Tbsp. chopped green onion. Place ¼ lb. of pork mixture on top of the stuffing and use the classic press to seal.

Cook over direct heat until thoroughly cooked. Serve burger on bun garnished with sour cream dressing.

Yield: 2 stuffed burgers

STUFFED MEDITERRANEAN-STYLE BURGER WITH TZATZIKI

Take your taste buds on a journey to the Mediterranean with this rich beef-and-lamb burger. Served on flatbread, stuffed with feta cheese and olives, and topped with tangy tzatziki, these burgers bring home the zest of the Greek isles.

Ingredients:

- ¾ lb. ground beef, 85/15%
- ¾ lb. ground lamb
- 2 Tbsp. red wine
- 2 Tbsp. fresh oregano, chopped
- 1 tsp. fresh mint, chopped
- 1 garlic clove, finely chopped
- Salt and pepper, to taste
- 4 oz. feta cheese, crumbled
- 2 Tbsp. red onion, chopped
- 2 Tbsp. Kalamata olives, pitted and chopped
- ½ c. tzatziki sauce
- 2 flatbreads, grilled

Method:

Combine ground beef, ground lamb, red wine, oregano, mint, garlic, salt, and pepper to taste in mixing bowl, using hands to mix thoroughly. To form burgers, place ½ lb. of ground meat mixture into the ring of the burger press. Use the classic press to form the base patty, then push the slider press into the patty to form a well. Stuff the burger with 2 oz. crumbled feta, 1 Tbsp. red onion, and 1 Tbsp. Kalamata olives. Place ¼ lb. of ground meat mixture on top of the stuffing and use the classic press to seal. Cook over direct heat until thoroughly cooked. Serve burger on grilled flatbread garnished with tzatziki.

Yield: 2 stuffed burgers

MUSHROOM AND ROASTED PEPPER STUFFED BURGER

This earthy, mushroom-stuffed burger is rich in hearty flavors, livened up by refreshing arugula and red pepper. Whole-grain mustard and a poppy-seed bun round out the delicious harvest.

Ingredients:

1 c. mushrooms, sliced
1 Tbsp. olive oil
1½ lbs. ground beef, 85/15%
Salt and pepper, to taste
4 oz. fontina cheese, grated

½ c. roasted red peppers, sliced
2 Tbsp. whole grain mustard
1 c. arugula
2 poppy seed buns

Method:

Heat a sauté pan over medium heat. Add olive oil and sauté sliced mushrooms until golden brown. Season with salt and pepper to taste. Set aside to cool. Combine ground beef, salt, and pepper to taste in mixing bowl, using hands to mix thoroughly.

To form burgers, place ½ lb. of ground beef mixture into the ring of the burger press. Use the classic press to form the base patty, then push the slider press into the patty to form a well. Stuff the burger with 2 oz. fontina cheese, 2 Tbsp. mushrooms, and 1 Tbsp. roasted red pepper. Place ¼ lb. of beef mixture on top of the stuffing and use the classic press to seal.

Cook over direct heat until thoroughly cooked. Serve burger on poppy seed bun garnished with whole grain mustard, arugula, more roasted red peppers, and mushrooms.

Yield: 2 stuffed burgers

BEEF SLIDERS WITH MUSHROOMS & SMOKED GOUDA

Smoky Gouda smothers these simple yet succulent sliders. The powerful cheese flavor pairs well with the sautéed mushrooms, resulting in sliders that will disappear like magic.

Ingredients:

1 lb. ground beef, 85/15%
2 c. cremini mushrooms, sliced thinly
3 slices smoked Gouda, cut in half and folded into small squares
6 slider buns
Salt and pepper, to taste
Olive oil, for cooking
¼ c. mayonnaise
1 c. arugula

Method:

Slice cremini mushrooms and sauté in a medium pan until soft and fragrant. Divide meat into six equal pieces and form patties using small press. Season patties with salt and pepper then brush with olive oil. Cook patties on the grill over direct flame 2-3 minutes per side or until desired doneness is achieved, adding cheese during the last 30 seconds. Serve sliders topped with mayo, mushrooms, and arugula.

Yield: 6 sliders

BUFFALO CHICKEN SLIDERS WITH CRISPY SHALLOTS

Buffalo wings without the bones! These sliders are perfect for a Game Day party: an elevated finger food with less mess but even more flavor.

Ingredients:

1 lb. ground chicken, thigh meat

¼ c. Buffalo sauce

¼ c. ranch dressing

1 head butter lettuce

3 slices Swiss cheese, cut in half and folded into small squares

6 slider buns

Salt and pepper, to taste

Olive oil, for cooking

Crispy Shallots

1 c. buttermilk

1 c. all-purpose flour

1 c. light olive oil, for frying

Method:

Divide chicken meat into six equal pieces and form patties using small press. Season patties with salt and pepper then brush with olive oil. Slice shallots into thin rings. Pour buttermilk into a small bowl. Dredge shallots in flour, place into the buttermilk, then dredge again in flour. Place olive oil in a sturdy-bottomed pan and preheat olive oil to 375°F on the stovetop. Once the oil is hot, fry the shallots until golden brown. Season with a light sprinkling of salt immediately after cooking.

Cook patties on the grill over direct flame 3-4 minutes per side until cooked through, basting with buffalo sauce as the patties cook. Melt cheese during final 30 seconds cooking patties. Serve sliders with lettuce, ranch dressing, and additional buffalo sauce.

Yield: 6 sliders

BACON 'N EGG BREAKFAST SLIDERS WITH CHIPOTLE MAYO

Burgers for brunch? Bring it on! These mini burgers use beloved breakfast staples to their advantage – who doesn't love bacon and eggs? – and the chipotle mayo is sure to wake you up!

Ingredients:

1 lb. ground beef, 85/15%

3 large eggs

6 slices bacon

3 slices cheddar cheese, cut in half and folded into small squares

3 Tbsp. chives

1 can chipotle chilies, in adobo sauce

¼ c. mayonnaise

6 slider buns

Salt and pepper, to taste

Method:

Remove the seeds from one chipotle chili and mince it finely. Add minced chili to the mayonnaise along with 1 tsp. of adobo sauce. Mix well to combine. Mince chives and set aside.

Divide meat into six equal pieces and form patties using small press. Season patties with salt and pepper then brush with olive oil. Cook bacon strips in a sturdy-bottomed pan until fully cooked; set aside. Cook patties on the grill over direct flame 2-3 minutes per side or until desired doneness is achieved, adding cheese during the last 30 seconds. In a small non-stick pan, gently scramble eggs until desired consistency is reached. Serve sliders topped with bacon, eggs, chives, and chipotle mayo.

Yield: 6 sliders

HOISIN PORK SLIDERS WITH ASIAN SLAW

Satisfy your craving for Asian flavors with a burger, not a white cardboard box! These sliders are perked up with ginger and brushed with hoisin sauce; a cabbage and carrot slaw tops your creation with cool crunch.

Ingredients:

1 lb. ground pork
1 tsp. ginger powder
¼ c. hoisin sauce
6 slider buns
Salt and pepper, to taste
Olive oil, for cooking

Slaw:

1 c. napa cabbage, shredded
½ c. carrot, shredded
3 Tbsp. rice vinegar
1 Tbsp. sesame oil
½ tsp. salt
½ tsp. sugar
¼ c. mayonnaise

Method:

Combine all slaw ingredients in a small non-reactive bowl, mix thoroughly, and allow to marinate at least 30 minutes before preparing patties. Place ground pork into a medium-sized bowl, add ginger powder and mix to combine. Divide meat into six equal pieces and form patties using small press. Season patties with salt and pepper then brush with olive oil.

Cook patties on the grill over direct flame 2-3 minutes per side or until desired doneness is achieved, brushing with hoisin sauce while cooking. Serve sliders topped with mayonnaise and slaw.

Yield: 6 sliders

CARAMELIZED ONION & SWISS SLIDERS

These onion-topped sliders are so good you'll shed a few tears! Caramelized until translucent and sweet, yellow onions crown beef patties and Swiss cheese for fragrant and unforgettable burgers.

Ingredients:

- 1 lb. ground beef, 85/15%
- 1 yellow onion, halved and sliced into strips
- 3 slices Swiss cheese, cut in half and folded into small squares
- 6 slider buns
- Salt and pepper, to taste
- Olive oil, as needed for cooking
- ¼ c. mayonnaise

Method:

Place onions in a sturdy-bottomed pan over medium heat and sauté until caramelized (25-30 minutes).

Divide meat into six equal pieces and form patties using small press. Season patties with salt and pepper then brush with olive oil. Cook patties on the grill over direct flame 2-3 minutes per side or until desired doneness is achieved, adding cheese during the last 30 seconds. Serve sliders topped with mayo and caramelized onions.

Yield: 6 sliders

A special thanks to all The Companion Group® Berkeley office taste testers
for trying so many burgers and giving great feedback.

Thanks to all of our contributors:
Wendy Boeger, Niki Gross, Sharon Kallenberger, & Tonatzin Ogunleye

Photography & Food Styling: Tiffany Threets, Nick Wellhausen, & Sharon Kallenberger

Book Design: Tiffany Threets & Diana Ghermann

Recipes: Nick Wellhausen & Sarah Goodwin

Copy: Simone Chavoor & Nick Wellhausen